A Call to Repentance & Restoration

A PERSONAL PRAYER GUIDE

INCLUDING A SOLEMN ASSEMBLY CEREMONY

Michael L. Rossmann

XULON PRESS

Xulon Press
2301 Lucien Way #415
Maitland, FL 32751
407.339.4217
www.xulonpress.com

Paperback ISBN-13: 978-1-6628-3167-6
eBook ISBN-13: 978-1-6628-3168-3

Table of Contents

Dedication

I would like to dedicate this book to my six grandchildren: Claire, Elynna, Preston, Alden, Gracie, and Corban. As the Nineveh Revival under Jonah's preaching allowed her to stand for more than a century longer allowing many more to come to true faith in the Messiah, may the Lord Jesus allow them to have a country in which He is honored yet again in their generation.

How to Use This Book

Part One: As A Personal Prayer Guide

1) What is this book? This book is first and foremost a personal prayer guide. To clearly present this, the second and third editions are divided into two parts. Part One is the personal prayer guide; Part Two a formal Solemn Assembly ceremony. I have redesigned Part One to address the needs of the individual who desires to respond to the Lord Jesus' call of repentance and restoration. Using this as a personal prayer guide, we, as individuals, can prepare our hearts to hear the Lord knocking on the door of the church and saying, "Behold, I stand at the door and knock. If anyone hears My voice and opens the door, I will come in to him and eat with him, and he with Me."[1]

2) This personal prayer guide is divided into four sections following the acronym of **P. R. A. Y.**: **P**raise the Lord for Who He is, *i.e.,* His character; **R**emember the wonderful deeds the Lord has done; **A**cknowledge our sins (individual, local and national) *and* our need for His Person, His grace, His mercy and His forgiveness; lastly, **Y**ield to the Life[2] of the Lord Jesus Christ afresh to empower us to accomplish His will on earth as it is done in heaven.

3) When this personal prayer guide is prayed in its entirety, it takes approximately 20–45 minutes. Of course, the Holy Spirit can guide you beyond any timetable.

4) When you come to the promptings for singing, I'm sure the Lord would love to hear you sing one of your favorite songs that appropriately represents the specific section.

5) Although all the prayers found in this ceremony are adapted from Scriptures, many are paraphrased and direct quotes of Scripture.[3] These are noted in the endnotes. Further, by placing these citations in the endnotes, the flow of this guide is maintained.

6) The endnotes of this personal prayer guide add depth and explanations for many of the respective sections of the book. It will be very beneficial if you familiarize yourself with them.

Part Two: As a Family or in a Small or Large Group for a Solemn Assembly Ceremony

1) Part Two of this book is the original ceremony to formally commemorate the Day of Atonement (*also called* The Feast of *Yom Kippur;* see Appendix A below for a brief discussion on this). Part Two of the book may also be used to facilitate any small group gathering that desires to seek the Lord's face in repentance and restoration.

2) This Ceremony follows the format of Part One (Noted in #2 above) but includes plural pronouns where appropriate. This is to facilitate the corporate call to repentance and restoration.

3) Note that it is helpful starting this ceremony off with a few remarks on the flow of the ceremony followed by a quiet time for reflection. This can then be followed by the

blowing of the *shofar* to formally indicate the beginning of the ceremony.

4) Although there are five different leader assignments throughout the book, the pastor and/or leaders of your church may find it necessary or more convenient to have fewer. In any case, the leaders of your church will begin the ceremony. (See p. 15 for the start of the ceremony.)

5) Depending on the degree of the outpouring of the Holy Spirit, this ceremony can be completed in 45 minutes to an hour. Obviously, the Holy Spirit is not limited to this time frame.[4]

6) Though this ceremony is called a "Solemn Assembly," this "solemn" need not be *dour*, but it does need to be sober. The Apostle Peter reminds us: "The end of all things is at hand; therefore, be self-controlled and sober-minded for the sake of your prayers."[5] The Joy of the Lord may truly flow during this time.[6] To encourage this, there are several places for praise songs of joy and thanksgiving.

7) These opportunities for singing can be easily coordinated with the music leaders of your church.[7] Songs appropriate for each section can be chosen to facilitate this call to repentance and reconciliation: Section One, **P**raise, concludes (p. 18) with an opportunity to sing praises; Section Two, **R**emember, concludes (p. 20) with the Doxology, but some other praise song may be substituted here; Section Four, **Y**ield, (p. 27) has an interlude opportunity for a praise song or two; the ceremony then concludes (p. 29) with a song or songs of dedication.

8) It is possible that during the ceremony some may be overcome with deep emotions and may need a private place to freely express these. If your facility has the availability, other rooms may be designated for such an outpouring.

14) Although the prayers in this ceremony may be prayed as a group in unison, they may also be prayed creatively, *e.g.*, responsively, or even alternating between sides of the facility (i.e., left, center, right), or men, women, children. Again, be creative.

15) As noted above, Appendix A below offers a brief overview of the Day of Atonement. Other sources noted in the endnotes may be used to get a more detailed understanding.[8]

16) Again, this personal prayer guide and Solemn Assembly Ceremony may be used at any time your church feels the prompting of the Holy Spirit, hearing the voice of Jesus through the door He is knocking on:

"Behold, I stand at the door and knock. If anyone hears My voice and opens the door, I will come in to him and eat with him, and he with Me." [9]

Introduction

This is not another book *about* prayer. It is a book *of* prayers. Books *about* prayer serve a vital role in motivating many to pray. In line with this, I have strongly felt a very heavy burden to teach people *how* to pray, meaning what words or Scriptures can be used to pray. Many have come to me in desperation saying, "I don't know *what* to pray." They seem to have no words to capture the cry of their heart. True, prayer is like talking to a friend. But sometimes even when talking with a friend, we are indeed speechless.

I'm sure you understand, as I do, that the Holy Spirit intercedes "with groans that words cannot express,"[10] but we also know the Lord Jesus taught His disciples to pray. This is where this book fits in. I believe it fills the gap for those who do not know where to begin to pray. It links words and Scriptures to the cries of all our hearts.

And what are the cries of our heart? Some are crying out for reformation. The church needs to boldly stand against the tide of an ever-encroaching enemy. Some are crying out for revival but have been discouraged by the deafness around them.

In His letter to the seven churches in the Revelation, our Risen Lord Jesus dictated to the Apostle John seven urgent messages to His People. These letters presented a very sobering call to "Repent!"[11] Except for Smyrna and Philadelphia, the other five churches had serious sins of which to repent. Although a few had some positive aspects, the Lord Jesus leveled against them some serious charges of some heinous and deadly sins. These required their urgent attention. I find the status of the church in the United States is no different.

Perhaps you are feeling the way I do: It is time we stop complaining about the sin in our culture and start offering a solution. The solutions may be many, but whatever solution we offer, I am sure we agree that it must begin with cleaning out our own house. It starts with personal repentance. When I repent, the Light of Jesus shines brighter in and through my life. And when you and I *both* repent, the Light of Jesus shines brighter still. It is *His* brilliance that changes lives. It is *His* brilliance that convicts other followers of Jesus. It is *His* brilliance that transforms us to live lives that truly reflect *Him*. And it is *His* brilliance that will ultimately influence those around us, even transforming our culture.

It is in this hope that I present this *Personal Prayer Guide*. It is a tool for those who find words difficult to capture their heart's desire to respond to the call to repentance and restoration. It is a tool for those who have just started following Jesus to light their path to a deeper intimacy with Him. It is a tool for the seasoned follower of Jesus to laser-focus their prayer life. May this tool become worn out from frequent use to the LORD's brilliance.

Part One

Overview

This Part One, A Personal Prayer Guide, follows the general pattern found in the Lord's letters to the seven churches: Praise; Problem; Promise. Along with this, the acronym, P. R. A. Y., is followed: **P**raise, **R**emember, **A**cknowledge and **Y**ield. (This pattern can be seen in the prayers of Nehemiah and Daniel as well.) As you feel the humble responsibility of answering the Lord's call to repentance and restoration, let us approach this in three areas:[12]

▶ Our personal relationship with the Great I AM through the Lord Jesus Christ

▶ Our personal relationships with our natural family & our supernatural family, the church

▶ Our relationships with others: Our community, our nation, and the world

Expanding on this pattern and acronym, P. R. A. Y.:

1) **Praise**—In song and in word, we will praise the LORD for Who He is.

2) **Remember**—In testimony and in Scripture, we will remember the good things the LORD has done for us.

3) **Acknowledge**—We acknowledge our need for the Lord Jesus Christ through confession. Allow yourself some quiet time for personal reflection and confession.[13]

4) **Yield**—This aspect presents an opportunity to actively yield to the Lord Jesus Christ's Life. This is done through prayer and quiet reflection. For example, we may pray a simple prayer like, "Lord Jesus Christ, be in me the man/woman of God You have designed me to be," and then go say or do (or not say & do) what He has prompted you to do. (Remember, you are "God's workmanship created in Christ Jesus to do good works" that He has prepared *in advance* for you to do.[14] So, empowered by the Lord Jesus Christ and through His Holy Spirit: Go do them.)

Preparation: Pause and Reflect

Pause: Please quietly familiarize yourself with this book, especially Part One, as you prepare your heart to answer the Lord Jesus Christ's call to repentance and restoration.

Reflect: One way to quiet ourselves before the Lord is to quietly reflect on specific Scriptures. This is the silent side of prayer— our listening to the Lord. Allow the Lord to speak to you as you read your favorite Psalms or other praise passages. (For example: Psalms 1, 8, 19, 29, 30, 33, 34, 48, 104, 111,145-150; 1 Chronicles 16:7-36; Revelation 2, 3, 4:11)

Answering the Call

I. PRAISE: Celebration & Adoration

- **Affirmation of Your Commitment to the Lord Jesus Christ**

Heavenly Father, I desire to come into Your presence. I confess that I want the Living Water, the Lord Jesus Christ. Hear my personal confession of faith:

I confess that I have received the Lord Jesus Christ and that I have repented of my sins. I confess that I have forsaken my past and have given to You my present and my future. I thank You that You have saved me by the Lord Jesus Christ's shed blood, that You have cleansed me from all unrighteousness, and that You have made me whole. I affirm that I have been saved by grace through faith. I acknowledge that You are my Lord, and I am Your child.

Heavenly Father, receive my praise: I extol You, I glorify You, I adore and worship You, the only true and living God, and Your only Begotten Son, Jesus Christ, our Lord, through the power of the Holy Spirit. Amen.

- **Sing a Song of Praise & Thanksgiving**

II. REMEMBER: Praise & Thanksgiving

- **Praise for all the LORD has done for you**

Heavenly Father, I praise You for all You have done for me. I am overwhelmed by a deep sense of thanksgiving and gratitude. I bless You and praise You for_____. [*Note the wonderful things the LORD has done for you.*]

- **Thanksgiving for all the Lord Jesus Christ is in you**

Heavenly Father, I thank You for making Lord Jesus Christ everything I will ever need. I praise You for the Lord Jesus Christ becoming my life. I acknowledge and affirm the truth that...

He is my Strength; He is my Wisdom; He is my Holiness; He is my Righteousness; He is my Redemption; He is my Peace; He is my Victory; He is my Joy; He is my Hope; He is my Spiritual Fullness.[15]

I acknowledge and affirm that the Lord Jesus Christ is my Life, my Head, and my Spiritual Mind.[16]

I put you on, Lord Jesus Christ, as my Spiritual Armor: I put You on as my Belt of Truth; my Breastplate of Righteousness; my Shield of Faith; my Helmet of Salvation; my Shoes of Peace.[17]

I put You on, Lord Jesus Christ, as my Spiritual Clothes: I put You on as my Hat of Humility; my Coat of Compassion; my Gloves of Kindness; my Socks of Gentleness; my Slippers of Patience: The Left Slipper of Forbearance & the Right Slipper of Forgiveness; my Belt of Love.[18]

You are my Advocate defending me, my Refuge protecting me, and my Rest refreshing me. [19]

AMEN!

- **Sing the Doxology**

III. ACKNOWLEDGE: Repent & Confess

Heavenly Father, open my eyes to see and my ears to hear what the Holy Spirit is saying to me and my church. I acknowledge that the Lord Jesus Christ is the Head of my church. I acknowledge His lordship over my life. I renounce any claim of ownership on my part. This is Your church, not mine. I renounce any independent spirit, and I declare my full dependence on You and interdependence on my brothers and sisters in Christ. I renounce any and all desires or attempts to exert my own will through contentious arguing, manipulating, intimidating, dominating or passively resisting. I confess that I desire Your will not my will, Your ways not my ways, Your thoughts not my thoughts. I again confess Lord Jesus Christ as the Lord and Head of me and my church.

Heavenly Father, by the shed blood of Your Son, the Lord Jesus Christ, and through His power:

✝ I renounce Satan, all his works, and all his ways.

✝ I renounce forsaking my first love. I renounce tolerating false teaching and overlooking non-Christian beliefs and practices among our church members. I renounce tolerating sexual immorality among our church members.[20]

✝ I renounce my reputation for being alive when I am dead. I renounce my incomplete deeds. I renounce my disobedience to Your Word including the Great Commandments and the Great Commission.[21]

✟   I renounce my lukewarmness, being neither hot nor cold for Christ. I renounce my pride in false financial security that blinds me to my actual spiritual needs.

✟   I renounce any root of bitterness.

Lord Jesus Christ, You have said that You will build Your church and the gates of Hell will not stand against it.[22] You have also called Your church to repentance: to remember our first love,[23] to be faithful to the point of death,[24] to reject the sin of Bala'am and sexual immorality,[25] to wake up and strengthen what remains,[26] and to be either hot or cold.[27]

I do not want to give Satan a foothold[28] or let him take advantage of me.[29] Therefore, I now confess my sins and the sins of Your church in the confident hope that You will set me free to do Your will.

•   **A Quiet Moment of Personal Confession**

Preparation: *Take this time to review such passages as 1 Corinthians 5:9-11; Galatians 5:19f, Ephesians 4:25-5:21; Colossians 3:5-17. Allow the Holy Spirit to convict you of sin. Then use the prayers presented below to confess those sins which the Holy Spirit prompts. Note that these prayers may be repeated for each incident or sin the Lord recalls.*

Prayer of Confession: Heavenly Father, by the shed blood of Your Son, Lord Jesus Christ, and through His power, I confess *sinful act.* I have sinned against You, and I ask the Lord Jesus Christ to bear the consequences of my actions.[30] Lord Jesus Christ, remove the pain and shame that I have caused Your

Name and others. I ask You to be the part of my life that has been disobedient to You. I release myself into Your hands.

Prayer of Forgiveness: Heavenly Father, by the shed blood of Your Son, Lord Jesus Christ, and through His Power, I forgive[31] _person's name_ for _sinful act_. I ask You, Lord Jesus Christ, to bear the consequences of his/her actions. Lord Jesus Christ, remove the pain and shame s/he has caused Your Name and me. Be that part of my life that has been damaged by him/her. I release _person's name_ into Your hands.

IV. YIELD: Submit To & Be Empowered By The Lord Jesus Christ

Lord Jesus Christ, You desire to make me, as a part of Your church, holy. Cleanse me with the water of Your Word. Present me to Yourself as a part of Your radiant church without stain, wrinkle, or any other blemish. Present me to Yourself as holy and blameless.[32] I desire what You desire; I am to be holy because You are holy.[33] Lord Jesus Christ, be my holiness[34] so that I might stand against the schemes of the Enemy.[35]

Therefore, I ask You, as the Head of Your church, to remove, break, and extinguish[36] any attempt by the Enemy, his allies, or familiar or unclean spirits to harass, embarrass, discourage, distract, or otherwise delay or detour Your work in my life.

Heavenly Father, by the shed blood of Your Son, Lord Jesus Christ, and by His authority, I forgive each person who has hurt, disappointed, or frustrated me. I forgive myself for the foolish and sinful things I have done. I forgive as You forgive. I release any resentment or regrets into Your hands.

Because You alone can heal broken hearts and bind up wounds, I ask You to remove any bitterness I may harbor in my heart. Heal the pain and remove the shame in my heart.

I announce that I am Your child, Heavenly Father. I have been bought and made holy by the precious blood of the Lord Jesus Christ. I am empowered by the Holy Spirit, the Spirit of power, love, and a sound mind. I resist the Enemy and all his allies. I stand firm in my faith in the Lord Jesus Christ. Therefore, the Enemy and all his allies must flee from me.[37] They have no claim to me because I am the Lord Jesus Christ's holy possession. In His Authority, Amen.

Lord Jesus Christ, You have promised that no weapon formed against me will prosper, and no temptation will overtake me without You being the Way of escape.[38] I now make You my refuge so that no harm will befall me.[39] Fill me, Heavenly Father, with Your Holy Spirit, the Spirit of power, love and a sound mind.[40] Allow me to fulfill those works You have prepared for me in advance to do.[41]

- **Announcing Christ Jesus as My Fullness**

Heavenly Father, since I am in Your Son, the Lord Jesus Christ, by Your grace I now confess:[42]

I have been justified—completely forgiven of all my sins, redeemed, and made righteous; the debt against me has been canceled.[43]

Dying with the Lord Jesus Christ, sin no longer has power to rule over my life.[44]

I have been crucified with the Lord Jesus Christ. The life I now live is His Life.[45]

I find my life is now hidden with the Lord Jesus Christ in You, Heavenly Father. The Lord Jesus Christ is now my life.[46]

Since I have died, I no longer live for myself, but for Christ, and I have been raised up and seated with Christ in heaven.[47]

I am free forever from condemnation.[48]

I have been bought with a price; I am not my own; I belong to You, Heavenly Father.[49]

I have been rescued from the domain of Satan's rule and transferred to the kingdom of Your Son, Jesus.[50]

I have been adopted by You, Heavenly Father, to be Your child.[51]

I have freedom and confidence to approach You with boldness, coming before Your throne to find mercy and grace in time of need.[52]

I have been blessed with every spiritual blessing.[53]

I have been given the mind of Christ.[54]

I have been made complete in Christ.[55]

I have been made righteous in Christ.[56]

I have been given exceedingly great and precious promises by You by which I am a partaker of Your divine nature.[57]

Heavenly Father, sanctify me by Your Truth; Your Word is Truth. By the authority of the Lord Jesus Christ. Amen.

• **Sing a Song of Rejoicing**

- **A Prayer of Commitment** [58]

Lord Jesus Christ, make me an instrument of Your presence to bring healing and not harm as You increase the influence of Your Kingdom through me and Your church:

Where there is unrest ...be peace in me.
Where there is hatred ...be love in me.
Where there is injury... be pardon in me.
Where there is doubt... be faith in me.
Where there is despair ... be hope in me.
Where there is darkness ... be light in me.
Where there is sadness ... be joy in me.
Where there is foolishness ... be wisdom in me.
Where there is hypocrisy ... be sincerity in me.
Where there is indignation & contempt ... be respect in me
Where there is fear ... be courage in me.
Where there are lies... be Truth in me.
Lord Jesus Christ, grant that I may not so much seek:
to be consoled ...as to console;
    to be understood ... as to understand;
        to be loved ... as to love.

For:
It is in giving ... that we receive,
It is in pardoning ... that we are pardoned,
It is in dying to ourselves ...that Your eternal Life is manifested in us. Amen.

- **Sing a Song of Dedication**

Part Two

A Solemn Assembly Ceremony

Preparation: Pause and Reflect

Pause: Please quietly familiarize yourself with this ceremony as you prepare your heart to answer the Lord Jesus Christ's call to repentance and restoration.

Reflect: One way to quiet ourselves before the Lord is to quietly reflect on specific Scriptures. This is the silent side of prayer—our listening to the Lord. Allow the Lord to speak to you as you read your favorite Psalms or other praise passages. (Some suggestions: Psalms 1, 8, 19, 29, 30, 33, 34, 48, 104, 111,145-150; 1 Chronicles 16:7-36; Revelation 4:11.)

I. PRAISE: Celebration & Adoration

- **Invocation**
- **Sound the Shofar**

Leader A: Blow the trumpet in Zion, declare a holy fast, call a sacred assembly. Gather the people, consecrate the assembly; bring together the elders, gather the children, those nursing at the breast. Let the bridegroom leave his room and the bride her chamber. Let the priests, who minister before the LORD, weep between the temple porch and the altar. Let them say, [59]

Leader B: "Spare your people, O LORD. Do not make your inheritance an object of scorn, a byword among the nations. Why should they say among the peoples, 'Where is their God?'"[60]

Leader C: "Now, O Lord our God, who brought Your people out of Egypt with a mighty hand and who made for Yourself a name that endures to this day, we have sinned, we have done wrong. O Lord, in keeping with all Your righteous acts, turn away Your anger and Your wrath from Jerusalem, Your city, Your holy hill.[61]

Leader D: "Our sins and the iniquities of our fathers have made … Your people an object of scorn to all those around us. Now, our God, hear the prayers and petitions of Your servant. For Your sake, O LORD, look with favor on [us]. Give ear, O God, and hear; open Your eyes and see the desolation of the city that bears Your Name.[62]

Leader E: "We do not make requests of You because we are righteous, but because of Your great mercy. O Lord, listen! O Lord, forgive! O Lord, hear and act! For Your sake, O my God, do not delay because Your city and Your people bear Your Name."[63]

All the Leaders:[64] Thus says the LORD: "Come, all you who are thirsty, come to the waters; and you who have no money, come, buy and eat! Come, buy wine and milk without money and without cost. Why spend money on what is not bread, and your labor on what does not satisfy? Listen, listen to Me, and eat what is good, and your soul will delight in the richest of fare.

"Give ear and come to me; hear Me, that your soul may live. I will make an everlasting covenant with you, My faithful love promised to David.

"See, I have made him a witness to the peoples, a leader and commander of the peoples. Surely you will summon nations you know not, and nations that do not know you will hasten to you because of the LORD your God, the Holy One of Israel, for He has endowed you with splendor."

Leader E: Seek the LORD while He may be found; call on Him while He is near.

All Leaders: Let the wicked forsake his way and the evil man his thoughts. Let him turn to the LORD, and He will have mercy on him, and to our God, for He will freely pardon.

Leader D: "For My thoughts are not your thoughts, neither are your ways My ways," declares the LORD. "As the heavens are higher than the earth, so are My ways higher than your ways and My thoughts than your thoughts. As the rain and the snow come down from heaven, and do not return to it without watering the earth and making it bud and flourish, so that it yields seed for the sower and bread for the eater, so is My word that goes out from My mouth: It will not return to Me empty but will accomplish what I desire and achieve the purpose for which I sent it.

All Leaders: You will go out in joy and be led forth in peace; the mountains and hills will burst into song before you, and all the trees of the field will clap their hands."

- **Affirmation of our Commitment to the Lord Jesus Christ**

ALL: Heavenly Father, we desire to come into Your presence. We confess that we want the Living Water, the Lord Jesus Christ. Hear our personal confession of faith:

We confess we have received the Lord Jesus Christ and we have repented of our sins. We confess we have forsaken our past and have given to You our present and our future. We thank You that You have saved us by the Lord Jesus Christ's shed blood, that You have cleansed us from all unrighteousness, and that You have made us whole. We affirm we have been saved by grace through faith. We acknowledge that You are our Lord, and we are Your children.

Heavenly Father, receive our praise: We extol You, we glorify You, we adore and worship You, the only true and living God, and Your only Begotten Son, Jesus Christ, our Lord, through the power of the Holy Spirit. Amen.

- **Sing Songs of Praise & Thanksgiving**

II. REMEMBER: Praise & Thanksgiving

Leader A: As a church, what are we doing well; what would be commended by the Lord Jesus? Come share with the church family the marvelous acts the Lord has blessed us with. [*An open microphone may be provided for this.*]

- **Confession of our Position in Christ Jesus**

ALL: Heavenly Father, since the Lord Jesus Christ has become our life, we acknowledge and affirm the truth that...

He is our Strength; He is our Wisdom; He is our Holiness; He is our Righteousness; He is our Redemption; He is our Peace; He is our Victory; He is our Joy; He is our Hope; He is our Spiritual Fullness.[65]

We acknowledge and affirm that the Lord Jesus Christ is our Life, our Head, and our Spiritual Mind.[66]

We put you on, Lord Jesus Christ, as our Spiritual Armor: We put You on as our Belt of Truth; our Breastplate of Righteousness; our Shield of Faith; our Helmet of Salvation; our Shoes of Peace.[67]

We put You on, Lord Jesus Christ, as our Spiritual Clothes: We put You on as our Hat of Humility; our Coat of Compassion; our Gloves of Kindness; our Socks of Gentleness; our Slippers of Patience: The Left Slipper of Forbearance & the Right Slipper of Forgiveness; our Belt of Love.[68]

You are our Advocate defending us, our Refuge protecting us, and our Rest refreshing us. [69]

Thank You, Heavenly Father, for making Lord Jesus Christ everything we will ever need. AMEN!

- **Sing the Doxology (or some other praise song)**

III. ACKNOWLEDGE: Repent & Confess

Leader B: What problems does our Lord Jesus see in our midst?[70] What "things" hinder us or what sins easily entangle us?[71] Whatever they may be, we need to confess them and repent of them. There are two aspects of this confession. The first is confession of those sins *we* have committed or omitted. The second is confession of those who have sinned against us. Each is important in and of itself. The order, however, is to be determined by the Holy Spirit.[72] (The following prayers are for corporate sins. Part One Section III: Acknowledge can be used for individual sins.) First, let us pray together.

ALL: Heavenly Father, open our eyes to see and our ears to hear what the Holy Spirit is saying to our church and the churches of [our region]. We acknowledge that the Lord Jesus Christ is the Head of our church. We acknowledge His lordship over our lives and His body here at [your church's name]. We renounce any claim of ownership on our part. This is Your church, not ours. We renounce any independent spirit and declare our full dependence on You and interdependence on each other. We renounce all desires or attempts to exert our own wills through contentious arguing, manipulating, intimidating, dominating or passively resisting. We confess that we desire Your will not our will, Your ways not our ways, Your thoughts not our thoughts. We confess Lord Jesus Christ as the Lord and Head of [your church's name].

Heavenly Father, by the shed blood of Your Son, the Lord Jesus Christ, and through His power:

☩ We renounce Satan, all his works, and all his ways.

✞ We renounce forsaking our first love.

✞ We renounce tolerating false teaching, and overlooking non-Christian beliefs and practices among our members.

✞ We renounce tolerating sexual immorality among our members.[73]

✞ We renounce our reputation for being alive when we are dead.

✞ We renounce our incomplete deeds.

✞ We renounce our disobedience to Your Word including the Great Commandments and the Great Commission.[74]

✞ We renounce our lukewarmness, being neither hot nor cold for Christ.

✞ We renounce our pride in false financial security that blinds us to our actual spiritual needs.

✞ We renounce any root of bitterness.

Lord Jesus Christ, You have said that You will build Your church and the gates of Hell will not stand against it.[75] You have also called Your church to repentance: to remember our first love,[76] to be faithful to the point of death,[77] to reject the sin of Bala'am and sexual immorality,[78] to wake up and strengthen what remains,[79] and to be either hot or cold.[80]

We do not want to give Satan a foothold[81] or let him take advantage of us.[82] Therefore, we now confess our sins and the sins of Your church in the confident hope that You will set us free to do Your will.

• **A Quiet Moment of personal reflection & confession**

Leader C: Take this time to corporately confess those sins which the Holy Spirit suggests. Perhaps in addition to the above references, such passages as 1 Corinthians 5:9-11; Galatians 5:19f; Ephesians 4:25-5:21; Colossians 3:5-17 will allow the Holy Spirit to convict us of sin. [*Note: These prayers may be repeated as often as necessary.*]

Confession of Sins Prayer
Heavenly Father, by the shed blood of Your Son, Lord Jesus Christ, and through His Power, we confess *sinful act.* We have sinned against You, and we ask the Lord Jesus Christ to bear the consequences of our actions.[83] Lord Jesus Christ, remove the pain and shame we have caused Your Name and others. We ask You to be the part of our life that has been disobedient to You. We release ourselves into Your hands.

Forgiveness of Others Prayer
Heavenly Father, by the shed blood of Your Son, Lord Jesus Christ, and through His Power, we forgive[84] *person's name* for *sinful act*. We ask You, Lord Jesus Christ, to bear the consequences of his/her actions. Lord Jesus Christ, remove the pain and shame s/he has caused Your Name and us. Be that part of our life that has been damaged by him/her. We release *person's name* into Your hands.

[*After all have finished confessing and forgiving, Leaders D & E will lead in the following prayers, respectively*]

IV. YIELD: Submit To & Empowered By The Lord Jesus Christ

Leader D: Lord Jesus Christ, You desire to make us, Your church, holy. Cleanse us with the water of Your Word. Present us to Yourself as a radiant church without stain, wrinkle, or any other blemish. Present us to Yourself as holy and blameless.[85] We desire what You desire; we are to be holy because You are holy.[86] Lord Jesus Christ, be our holiness[87] so that we might stand against the schemes of the Enemy.[88]

Therefore, we ask You, as the Head of Your church, to remove, break, and extinguish[89] any attempt by the Enemy, his allies, or familiar or unclean spirits to harass, embarrass, discourage, distract, or otherwise delay or detour Your work through our fellowship here at [your church's name].

ALL: Heavenly Father, by the shed blood of Your Son, Lord Jesus Christ, and by His authority, we forgive each person who has hurt, disappointed, or frustrated our church or us. We forgive ourselves for the foolish and sinful things we have done. We forgive as You forgive us. We release any resentment or regrets into Your hands.

Because You alone can heal our broken hearts and bind up our wounds, we ask You to remove any bitterness we may harbor in our hearts. Heal the pain and remove the shame in our hearts and in the corporate memory of our church.

We announce that we are Your children, Heavenly Father. We have been bought and made holy by the precious blood of the Lord Jesus Christ. We are empowered by the Holy Spirit, the

Spirit of power, love, and a sound mind. We resist the Enemy and all his allies. We stand firm in our faith in the Lord Jesus Christ. Therefore, the Enemy and all his allies must flee from us.[90] They have no claim to us because we are the Lord Jesus Christ's holy possession. In His Authority, Amen.

Lord Jesus Christ, You have promised that no weapon formed against us will prosper, and no temptation will overtake us without You being the Way of escape.[91] We now make You our refuge so that no harm will befall us.[92] Fill us, Heavenly Father, with Your Holy Spirit, the Spirit of power, love and a sound mind.[93] Allow us to fulfill those works You have prepared for us in advance to do.[94]

Leader E: Announcing Christ Jesus as our Fullness

ALL: Heavenly Father, since I am in Your Son, the Lord Jesus Christ, by Your grace I now confess:[95]

I have been justified—completely forgiven of all my sins, redeemed, and made righteous; the debt against me has been canceled.[96]

Dying with the Lord Jesus Christ, sin no longer has power to rule over my life.[97]

I have been crucified with the Lord Jesus Christ. The life I now live is His Life.[98]

I find my life is now hidden with the Lord Jesus Christ in You, Heavenly Father. The Lord Jesus Christ is now my life.[99]

Since I have died, I no longer live for myself, but for Christ, and I have been raised up and seated with Christ in heaven.[100]

I am free forever from condemnation.[101]

I have been bought with a price; I am not my own; I belong to You, Heavenly Father.[102]

I have been rescued from the domain of Satan's rule and transferred to the kingdom of Your Son, Jesus.[103]

I have been adopted by You, Heavenly Father, to be Your child.[104]

I have freedom and confidence to approach You with boldness, coming before Your throne to find mercy and grace in time of need.[105]

I have been blessed with every spiritual blessing.[106]

I have been given the mind of Christ.[107]

I have been made complete in Christ.[108]

I have been made righteous in Christ.[109]

I have been given exceedingly great and precious promises by You by which I am a partaker of Your divine nature.[110]

Heavenly Father, sanctify us by Your Truth; Your Word is Truth. By the authority of the Lord Jesus Christ. Amen.

- **Sing a Song of Rejoicing**

Prayers Of Empowerment & Restoration

Leader A: Faith is not passive, but active: By faith, Abraham *offered* his son, Isaac; by faith, Moses and the Israelites *passed through* the Red Sea on dry ground; by faith, the Jericho walls *fell down*; and by faith, we *walk* in the steps of our Savior. Let us rededicate our lives afresh to walk by faith:

ALL: Heavenly Father, we desire to walk by faith and not by sight. We desire to follow in the footsteps of Your Son, our Lord Jesus Christ. We rededicate our lives afresh to You this day. Since we have repented of our past, restore us that we might serve You more faithfully. Empower us to live the Life that is pleasing to You. Empower us by the Lord Jesus Christ's Life through the Holy Spirit in us and through us. In Jesus' Name. Amen.[111]

Leader B: And now by faith we commit our future to the LORD's will. Let us use the open microphone, once again, to answer the questions: What would Jesus have us do? What do we need to remember to return to our first love of Him? What new and bold "adventure" is He prompting us to step out in faith and achieve in His strength?

• **A Prayer of Commitment** [112]

Leader C: Join me in this prayer of commitment.

Lord Jesus Christ, make me an instrument of Your presence to bring healing and not harm as You increase the influence of Your Kingdom through me, (our church and our various ministries):

Where there is unrest …be peace in me.
Where there is hatred …be love in me.
Where there is injury… be pardon in me.
Where there is doubt… be faith in me.
Where there is despair … be hope in me.
Where there is darkness … be light in me.
Where there is sadness … be joy in me.
Where there is foolishness … be wisdom in me.
Where there is hypocrisy … be sincerity in me.
Where there is noise … be silence in me.
Where there is indignation & contempt … be respect in me
Where there is fear … be courage in me.
Where there are lies… be Truth in me.
Lord Jesus Christ, grant that I may not so much seek:
    to be consoled …as to console;
        to be understood … as to understand;
            to be loved … as to love.

For:
    It is in giving … that we receive,
    It is in pardoning … that we are pardoned,
    It is in dying to ourselves …that Your eternal Life is manifested in us. Amen.

- **Sing a Song of Dedication**

- **Benediction**

Appendix

For several years now I have presented at our church in Grand Junction an opportunity to respond to our Lord Jesus' call to repentance and restoration. I have used the Day of Atonement (*aka Yom Kippur*) as a model for such. Since the Lord Jesus is not only our Passover Lamb,[113] but also our atoning sacrifice,[114] it seems proper to do this. Thus, we annually observe the Day of Atonement commemorating the Lord Jesus Christ as our atoning sacrifice[115] using this Personal Prayer Guide in Part One and the Solemn Assembly Ceremony in Part Two.

The Day of Atonement is the second of the Fall Feasts the LORD commanded Israel to commemorate. This is found in Leviticus 23:26-32. (The details of how to honor this Feast are found in Leviticus chapter 16.) The LORD commanded Israel through this Fall Feast to pause on this Holy Sabbath and reflect on their individual sins and the sins of their nation. With the High Priest interceding for the nation, two goats were prepared. One goat was slaughtered; its blood brought into the Holy of Holies. This symbolized the payment for their sins.[116] Through this act, the sins of the people were covered. After this, the High Priest laid his hands on the second goat, confessed the sins of the people, and sent it out into the wilderness. There it carried the sins of the nation, wandering until it died. This symbolized the separation of the sins from the people.[117]

Through this Feast, the sins of Israel where *covered*, but in the Messiah, the Lord Jesus, our sins are *removed*—taken away. This is what makes John the Baptist proclamation of Lord Jesus so profound: "Behold, the Lamb of God, who *takes away* the sin of the world!"[118] The Lord Jesus, as our atoning sacrifice doesn't merely cover our sins: He takes them *away!*[119]

As the Day of Atonement facilitates the call to repentance and restoration for the Nation of Israel, so too, may this *Personal Prayer Guide* and *the Solemn Assembly Ceremony* facilitate this call to repentance and restoration for you personally, for those gathered with you, and for the Body of Christ at large. Let us come before the HOLY ONE to confess our sins and praise Him for the ultimate sacrifice for our sins—the Lord Jesus Christ.[120]

Acknowledgments

This third edition has some minor syntax revisions, but still follows the majority of the second edition. With our church annually using this ceremony, I have discovered that these changes assisted in a smoother flow of the ceremony. There have also been some minor grammatically changes to assist in this flow as well. I am very grateful to the many who have faithfully used this book over the past few years as a supplement to their prayer life. They, too, have offered some helpful hints to improve this work.

The second edition was largely encouraged by my dear wife, Kathy, and my dear brother in the faith, Jim Daugherty. They spurred me on to rework this primarily for personal use. Although the first edition attempted to address a need for a particular ceremony, this edition is addressing an even deeper need for prayer. Both Kathy and Jim are fellow prayer warriors. And to them I am humbly grateful for their input and encouragement.

I do not want to ignore all who helped in the first edition. As noted in the first edition, many eyes and hands have seen and touch the preliminary forms of this book. Much of the material in this book has been deeply influenced by my mentor, Bob Bingham. He set me on the pathway to freedom in the Lord Jesus Christ. My dear brothers, Bob Stevens, Ed Harris, and

Doug Sikes have lent their theological perspectives to the mix. Ed Harris provided the soundboard and cattle prod I needed to get this to the press. Two of my daughters, Ashley and Crystal, also had a major input in the editing, word choices and flow of the text. My third daughter, Bethany, was a constant encouragement, keeping me on task. All this said, I am humbly grateful for all these, and though I have read, reread, and nearly memorized each word, I am still humbly aware of my responsibility for any misspellings or missed Scripture addresses.

About the Author

Michael grew up in a very faithfully religious home where both his parents taught religious education. This laid a strong foundation for his coming to the Lord Jesus in the early 70's during the Jesus People Movement. His strong love for Jesus grew like a fire within him. He couldn't contain it. Many called him a Jesus Freak. He started sharing the Lord with all he met or lived with in the dorms at Arizona State University. While there, he joined Dr. Michael Schiffman, who started a ministry to Jewish people called, "The Young Lions of Judah," which later merged with the Chosen People Ministry.

After receiving his BS degree from Arizona State University, Michael remained on campus becoming the campus director for Chosen People Ministries. While on campus, he started a Christian Awareness Week, organized a prayer group uniting the various Christian campus ministries, and formed a Christian Music band named, Sardis. He played acoustic and electric rhythm guitar, and, Kathy, his new wife, played flute in the band.

In 1980, Michael and Kathy moved for Michael to attend Denver Seminary, where he received a Master of Divinity with honors. He stayed in the Denver area and worked at a local church as an associate pastor. He taught Bible Studies, coached basketball & softball, wrote songs & poetry, and worked in Youth & Young Marrieds Ministries.

Michael and Kathy moved to Grand Junction, Colorado to be the pastor of a rural Evangelical Free church. Since 2000, he has faithfully served as the pastor of a nondenominational Bible church. He has been actively involved in the community through the Ministerial Alliance, ShareFest, coaching soccer and substitute teaching.

Over the years Michael has written several pamphlets on prayer, including *The Shepherd's Pathway to Wholeness*, *The Risen Warrior's Way*, and *CPR [Critical Prayer Resuscitation]: Devoted to Scriptural Praying*. He has taught theology and philosophy at Colorado Christian University. He has presented Messianic Passovers and Solemn Assemblies for churches and small groups for over 35 years. Michael and Kathy enjoy a close relationship with their three adult daughters and their six growing grandchildren. He still enjoys coaching soccer, gardening, playing guitar, and writing songs & poetry.

Endnotes

1   Revelation 3:20 (*The Holy Bible: English Standard Version.* Wheaton: Standard Bible Society, 2001. Print. Hereafter *ESV*) See also Luke 3:8 and Matthew 3:8.

2   You will notice that I use an upper case "L" (here and throughout the book) to describe this life that is in the Lord Jesus Christ. By using this upper case "L," I am distinguishing it from our "natural," earthy life. This upper case "L" Life is the born again, transformed, eternal Life that is in Him (John 1:4) and that is in us when we confess Jesus as Lord and believe in our hearts that He has been raised from the dead. See Romans 10:9-10; John 14:6; Colossians 3:4 as examples of the Lord Jesus being our Life.

3   Some will struggle with the written format of these prayers. I appreciate this. To me, ritualistic and vain repetitions come from a heart that is not wholly engaged in any prayer, be it from the "heart," the Scriptures or this book. Mindless reading is no more effective than a prayer wheel spinning in the wind. I pray that the Lord Jesus Christ will empower you through His Holy Spirit to pray these prayers from the heart. Being brought up in the Catholic church, I have always appreciated corporate, gathered praying. But I understand that many who were not brought up in this

tradition may not have the same freedom to pray written prayers, perhaps even thinking that the Holy Spirit cannot "inhabit" such praying. If one considers that praying the Scriptures is quite all right, and that much of this book is merely Scriptures being "prayed," perhaps the resistance or any hesitation will diminish or evaporate altogether. In any case, allow the Lord Jesus Christ to fill you with His Holy Spirit so to truly empower you to pray in the Spirit. Further, these prayers are formatted as guidelines to respond to the Lord's call to repentance and restoration. Whatever the case, when praying as a group, this book enhances the experience much like an ignition switch.

4   Nehemiah records for us that Israel read the Book of the Law from daybreak until noon during the Feast of Tabernacles (8:3), and 9:1ff records the outpouring of repentance. This being the case, let us be sensitive to the Holy Spirit's leading concerning time management.

5   1 Peter 4:7 (*ESV*) However, I am not implying that, "*The end*" is near, but I am noting that wherever we are on the Lord's timeline, we need to be praying. In order to do this, we need to be alert and sober. Though this soberness is serious, it need not squeeze out the Joy of the Lord.

6   Nehemiah 8:9-10 captures the leaders' exhortation culminating with: "…This day is sacred to our Lord. Do not grieve, for the joy of the LORD is your strength."

7   When presenting large Solemn Assemblies, I have discovered that presenting all the singing in the "Sing Songs of Praise & Thanksgiving" section on p. 18 enhances the flow of the ceremony dramatically. Whereas in smaller settings, following the presented ceremony works very well.

8   Kevin Howard and Marvin Rosenthal, *The Feasts of the Lord* (Thomas Nelson, 1997), pp. 188-133; Mitch & Zhava Glaser, *The Feasts of Israel* (Moody Press, 1987), pp. 77-154; Dr. Richard Booker, *Celebrating Jesus in the Biblical Feasts* (Destiny Image Publishers, 2009), pp. 125-139; Barney Kasdan, *God's Appointed Times* (Lederer Books 1993), pp. 77-89; Bruce R. Booker, *The Fall Feasts of Israel* CreateSpace Independent Publishing Platform, 2008), pp. 41-83.

9   Revelation 3:20 *ESV*

10 Romans 8:26-27

11 Interestingly enough, in the letter to the churches at Smyrna and Philadelphia, the Lord Jesus did not mention anything in need of repentance.

12 These are clearly patterned off the two greatest commandments: to love the Lord with all our being, and to love our neighbor as ourselves.

13 According to Matthew 18:15-20 and James 5:15-16, I believe that as public the sin, so public the confession, and as private the sin, so private the confession. This means that private sins are privately confessed in your heart. Whereas more public sins are confessed to the particular group aware of the sin. Lastly, sins that are obviously known by the "public" need to be confessed before the church. I trust the Holy Spirit will give us the discernment as to which is needed. (When using Part Two of this book as a group, a separate room or area in the church may be provided either for private prayer or for the small group of people you need to confess to. If the sin is "public," use the open microphone.)

14   Ephesians 2:10, emphasis added

15   This prayer is based on the following verses: Ps. 27:1, 1
     Corinthians 1:30, 2 Corinthians 5:21; Ephesians 2:14; Jn.
     16:33 1 Corinthians 15:57; Colossians 2:15, John 15:11,
     Colossians 1:27, Colossians 2:9, 10

16   Colossians 3:4; Ephesians 4:15; 1 Corinthians 2:16

17   Ephesians 6:10-18

18   I have built on the idea of "clothe yourselves" into the
     Clothes of Christ from Colossians 3:12-14. The trigger for
     these individual articles of clothing was the "Belt" of Love
     in v. 14.

19   This prayer is based on the following verses:1 John 2:1,
     Psalm 18:2, Mt. 11:28; Hebrews 4:10.

20   Once again, see Revelation 2-3

21   See Revelation 3:2 & Matthew 22:37-39; 28:18-20

22   Matthew 16:17-19

23   Revelation 2:4ff

24   Revelation 2:10; 3:10

25   Revelation 2:14f, 20ff

26   Revelation 3:2

27   Revelation 3:15

28   Ephesians 4:27

29   2 Corinthians 2:11

30   As we know, the wages of sin is death (Romans 6:23): This
     death is the *ultimate* consequence of our sins. The Lord
     Jesus has already paid this price, but there are more inter-
     mediate or temporal consequences. For example, one con-
     sequence of David's sin with Bathsheba is that the baby

died. Another consequence is the sword never departing from his household. (See 2 Samuel 12:7-12 for more.) All these consequences were to discipline David. (See Hebrews 12:7.) The Lord could have removed all the consequences, or He could have enforced them all. So, too, with us, if there is *any* consequence left behind, it is to discipline us, thus reminding us that the Lord truly does love us. Remember, Jesus still has the scars...

31   I phrase the prayer this way because only the Lord can truly forgive sins. We join His sacrifice on the cross, becoming dispensers of His Grace and Mercy by forgiving those who have wounded us—even if they may not have known what they were doing.

32   Ephesians 5:25-27

33   1 Peter 1:13-15

34   1 Corinthians 1:30

35   Ephesians 6:10f

36   Ephesians 6:16

37   James 4:7-10

38   Isaiah 54:17; 1 Corinthians 10:13

39   Psalm 91:10

40   2 Timothy 1:7

41   Ephesians 2:10

42   This list has been adapted from my mentor, Bob Bingham's, material and from Neil Anderson, *The Bondage Breaker*, (Eugene, Oregon: Harvest House Publishers, 1990, 1993 www.harvesthousepublishers.com), pp. 242-44.

43   Romans 5:1; Galatians 3:13, 14; Colossians 1:14; 2:14

44 Romans 6:6, 11

45 Galatians 2:20

46 Colossians 3:1-4

47 2 Corinthians 5:14, 15; Ephesians 2:6

48 Romans 8:1

49 1 Corinthians 6:19, 20

50 Colossians 1:13

51 Ephesians 1:5

52 Ephesians 3:12; Hebrews 4:16

53 Ephesians 1:3

54 1 Corinthians 2:16

55 Colossians 2:10

56 2 Corinthians 5:21

57 2 Peter 1:4

58 Adapted by Michael L. Rossmann from Francis of Assisi's *Prayer of Peace*

59 Joel 2:15-17a

60 Joel 2:17b

61 Daniel 9:15-16a

62 Daniel 9:16b-18a

63 Daniel 9:18b-19

64 The following Leaders' sections are from Isaiah 55:1-12.

65 This prayer is based on the following verses: Ps. 27:1, 1 Corinthians 1:30, 2 Corinthians 5:21; Ephesians 2:14; Jn. 16:33 1 Corinthians 15:57; Colossians 2:15, John 15:11, Colossians 1:27, Colossians 2:9, 10.

66 Colossians 3:4; Ephesians 4:15; 1 Corinthians 2:16

67 Ephesians 6:10-18

68 I have built on the idea of "clothe yourselves" into the Clothes of Christ from Colossians 3:12-14. The trigger for these individual articles of clothing was the "Belt" of Love in v. 14.

69 This prayer is based on the following verses:1 John 2:1, Psalm 18:2, Mt. 11:28; Hebrews 4:10.

70 This would be an appropriate time to read Revelation 2-3.

71 Hebrews 12:1

72 Again, rooms can be made available for personal privacy for confession and forgiveness.

73 Once again, see Revelation 2-3

74 See Revelation 3:2 & Matthew 22:37-39; 28:18-20

75 Matthew 16:17-19

76 Revelation 2:4ff

77 Revelation 2:10; 3:10

78 Revelation 2:14f, 20ff

79 Revelation 3:2

80 Revelation 3:15

81 Ephesians 4:27

82 2 Corinthians 2:11

83 As we know, the wages of sin is death (Romans 6:23): This death is the *ultimate* consequence of our sins. The Lord Jesus has already paid this price, but there are more intermediate or temporal consequences. For example, one consequence of David's sin with Bathsheba is that the baby

died. Another consequence is the sword never departing from his household. (See 2 Samuel 12:7-12 for more.) All these consequences were to discipline David. (See Hebrews 12:7.) The Lord could have removed all the consequences, or He could have enforced them all. So, too, with us, if there is *any* consequence left behind, it is to discipline us, thus reminding us that the Lord truly does love us. Remember, Jesus still has the scars...

84 I phrase the prayer this way because only the Lord can truly forgive sins. We join His sacrifice on the cross, becoming dispensers of His Grace and Mercy by forgiving those who have wounded us—even if they may not have known what they were doing.

85 Ephesians 5:25-27

86 1 Peter 1:13-15

87 1 Corinthians 1:30

88 Ephesians 6:10f

89 Ephesians 6:16

90 James 4:7-10

91 Isaiah 54:17; 1 Corinthians 10:13

92 Psalm 91:10

93 2 Timothy 1:7

94 Ephesians 2:10

95 This list has been adapted from my mentor, Bob Bingham's, material and from Neil Anderson, *The Bondage Breaker*, (Eugene, Oregon: Harvest House Publishers, 1990, 1993 www.harvesthousepublishers.com), pp. 242-44.

96 Romans 5:1; Galatians 3:13, 14; Colossians 1:14; 2:13-14

97 Romans 6:6, 11

98 Galatians 2:20

99 Colossians 3:1-4

100 2 Corinthians 5:14, 15; Ephesians 2:6

101 Romans 8:1

102 1 Corinthians 6:19, 20

103 Colossians 1:13

104 Ephesians 1:5

105 Ephesians 3:12; Hebrews 4:16

106 Ephesians 1:3

107 1 Corinthians 2:16

108 Colossians 2:10

109 2 Corinthians 5:21

110 2 Peter 1:4

111 This prayer is adapted from 2 Corinthians 5:7; 1 Peter 2:21; Matthew 26:39, 42; Jeremiah 15:19; Ephesians 4:1; Colossians 1:10, 28-29; Philippians 2:12-13.

112 Adapted by Michael L. Rossmann from Francis of Assisi's *Prayer of Peace.*

113 See 1 Corinthians 5:7

114 1 John 2:2

115 1 John 2:1f

116 See Leviticus 17:11 & Hebrews 9:22.

117 The Hebrew has two primary words for forgiveness. The first is *salach*. This carries the idea of pardoning or forgiving, in the sense of releasing the sin from the sinner.

Intriguingly, this word is only used of God as the source of this forgiveness. The other is *nasa* and connotes the lifting off and carrying away from the sinner the guilt and punishment of the particular sin. It is also interesting to note that there are two primary Greek words used for forgiveness. One word is *aphiēmi*, which basically means to divorce the sin from the person; the other word is *charizomai*, which basically means "freely give," thus walking in grace toward the forgiven 'sinner'. This is what our Lord does when He forgives us. Through His atoning sacrifice He has lifted up the guilt of our sin taking upon Himself the punishment we deserve. In doing this, He has *divorced* our sin from us, sending it away by burying it in the deepest ocean (Micah 7:19). He then continues to forgive us when we confess our sins as He then walks in grace towards us as forgiven. (See Colossians 2:13.)

118 John 1:29 ESV emphasis added.

119 Hebrews 9:22 explains that blood must be shed for forgiveness of sins. Jesus did this on Calvary as the goat that is slaughtered; and through this sacrifice He forgave us of *all* our sins (Colossians 2:13) placing them as far as the East is from the West (Psalm 103:12) and in this New Covenant He remembers our sins *no more* (Jeremiah 31:34).

120 See Leviticus 16 & 23:26-32; cf. Romans 3:25; Hebrews 1:3; 1 John 2:2.

CPSIA information can be obtained
at www.ICGtesting.com
Printed in the USA
LVHW090402031121
702256LV00004B/95

9 781662 831676